The Wonders of our World

Forests

Neil Morris

Crabtree Publishing Company

The Wonders of our World

Crabtree Publishing Company

350 Fifth Avenue,
Suite 3308
New York, New York
10118

360 York Road, R.R. 4
Niagara-on-the-Lake
Ontario
Canada LOS 1JO

73 Lime Walk
Headington
Oxford
England OX3 7AD

Author: Neil Morris
Managing editor: Jackie Fortey
Editors: Penny Clarke and Greg Nickles
Designer: Richard Rowan
Art director: Chris Legee
Picture research: Robert Francis

Picture Credits:
Artists: Martin Camm 11, 13, 20; Cecila Fitzsimons 8, 17 (bottom); Chris Forsey 27;
John Hutchinson 4; Deborah Johnson 17, 29; Paul Williams 11, 13, 18
Maps: AND Map Graphics Ltd.
Photographs: Canadian Pacific Railway 11; Robert Francis cover, 3, 4, 5, 9 (bottom),
14 (top), 15 (right), 17, 18, 19 (top), 23 (top left), 25 (bottom), 26 (bottom), 26-27,
28 (bottom), 29; Robert Harding Picture Library 7, 9 (top), 17 (bottom), 20-21,
22 (bottom right), 23 (bottom); Hutchison Picture Library 10, 12 (bottom), 14 (bottom),
15 (top and bottom left), 16 (bottom), 22 (top), 23 (top right), 24, 24-25, 27, 28 (top);
Caroline Jones 6; Sue Rose-Smith 25 (top); Science Photo Library 20;
All other photographs by Digital Stock and Digital Vision.

Cataloging-in-publication data

Morris, Neil
     Forests / Neil Morris.
p. cm. — (The wonders of our world)
Includes index.
ISBN 0-86505-833-4 (library bound) ISBN 0-86505-845-8 (pbk.)
Summary: Text and photographs examine various aspects of these
natural wonders including their formations, wildlife, and histories.
1. Forests and forestry—Juvenile literature. 2. Forest ecology—
Juvenile literature. [1. Forests and forestry. 2. Forest ecology.
3. Ecology.] I. Title. II. Series: Morris, Neil. Wonders of our
world.
QH86.M67 1998   j557.3   LC 98-10766 CIP

CONTENTS

WHAT IS A FOREST?

A FOREST is a large area of land that is thickly covered with trees. Smaller, less dense forests are called woods or woodlands.

Different types of forests grow in different climates and at different altitudes. The tropical rainforests for example, found in hot, rainy places near the equator, are different than the conifer forests of the world's cooler or more mountainous regions.

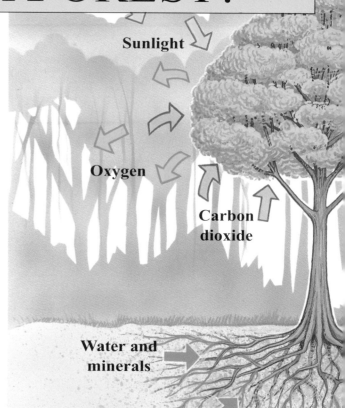

Sunlight

Oxygen

Carbon dioxide

Water and minerals

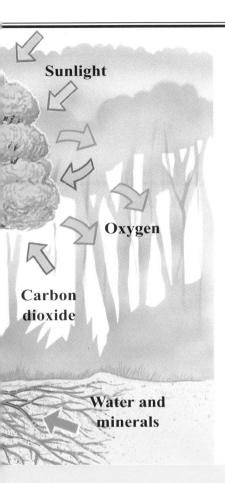

Sunlight

Oxygen

Carbon dioxide

Water and minerals

FOOD FOR TREES

Like all plants, the trees in a forest use sunlight to make their food (left). Chlorophyll, the green substance in their leaves, captures the energy in sunlight. Trees also take in carbon dioxide, a gas in the air, and mix it with water and minerals from the soil. During this process, trees give out the oxygen that animals and people need to breathe.

RAINFOREST MONKEYS

Forests are home to countless animals, such as capuchins (above). Capuchins live in the tropical forests of Central America, and spend most of their time high in the trees.

PLANT LIFE

Ferns and other small plants often cover the floor of a forest, such as the one in New Zealand shown left. In this cool, wet region, mosses and other plants grow on the trunks of the tall trees. All of these forest plants soak up a lot of rain. They stop the water from wearing away the soil and help prevent flooding.

CLEARING THE LAND

For thousands of years, people have been cutting down trees for timber. They have also cleared the land to make way for farms and towns. Now people are concerned, because vast areas of the world's forests are being destroyed.

WHERE IN THE WORLD?

FORESTS COVER more than a quarter of the earth's land area. They are found all over the world, except near the poles in the Arctic and Antarctic, and in deserts. In the polar regions, it is too cold for trees to grow, and in deserts, too dry.

Boreal forests stretch across northern Europe, Asia, and North America, where winters are harsh and summers are short. Temperate forests grow in mild regions, where there are warm summers and cool winters. Tropical forests are found near the equator, in the hottest part of the world.

THE WORLD'S FORESTS
Different kinds of forests grow in bands across the world (left).

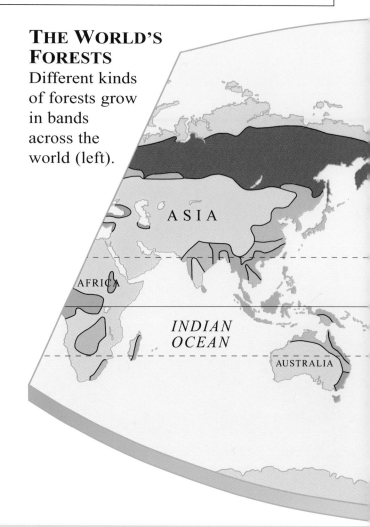

GUM TREES
Eucalyptus trees once grew only in Australian forests, such as the one shown left. Then people planted these tall, fast-growing trees in California, southern Europe, and other warm regions. Eucalyptus leaves contain gum and a valuable oil that is used in medicine.

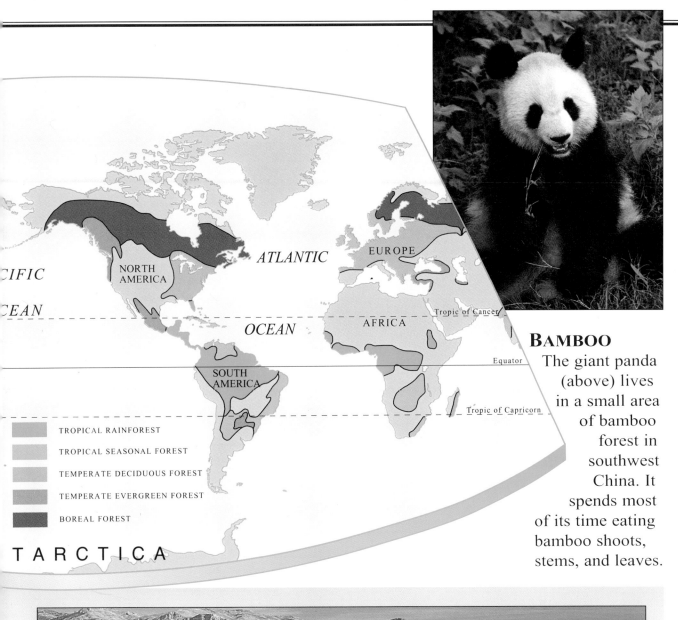

TROPICAL RAINFOREST
TROPICAL SEASONAL FOREST
TEMPERATE DECIDUOUS FOREST
TEMPERATE EVERGREEN FOREST
BOREAL FOREST

ATLANTIC

EUROPE

OCEAN

AFRICA

NORTH
AMERICA

SOUTH
AMERICA

PACIFIC

OCEAN

Tropic of Cancer

Equator

Tropic of Capricorn

TARCTICA

BAMBOO

The giant panda (above) lives in a small area of bamboo forest in southwest China. It spends most of its time eating bamboo shoots, stems, and leaves.

MEDITERRANEAN HILLS

IN areas with hot summers and mild winters, such as the lands around the Mediterranean Sea (right), tough, low bushes grow in place of tall trees. This hilly scrubland is in the southern part of Spain.

HOW FORESTS GREW

THE FIRST forests grew on marshy land hundreds of millions of years ago, when trees were like giant ferns. As the land dried out, new trees with needle-like leaves appeared. Over millions of years, the earth's climate changed, and forests of broad-leaf trees developed. In the Ice Ages, glaciers destroyed some of these forests, but the trees grew again when the ice melted.

SWAMP FORESTS

About 300 million years ago, the first forests (below) were full of tree ferns, club mosses, and horsetails. Amphibians came out of the water to live on land.

JURASSIC FORESTS
Dinosaurs (right) appeared 230 million years ago, and lived in the forests for 165 million years.

PREHISTORIC TREE TRUNK

THE stone trunk above is about 200 million years old. It is one of thousands in Petrified Forest National Park, in Arizona, USA. In prehistoric times, the forest was buried in volcanic ash, mud, and sand, which formed rocks. Wind and rain slowly wore away the rocks, leaving the tree trunks. These ancient trees were like pine trees.

COAL

IN the early swamp forests, layers of dead plants were buried in mud. Over millions of years, pressure turned the buried material into peat, and then into coal. The layers are easy to see at this open-cast coal mine in Australia (right).

IN THE NORTH

VAST FORESTS stretch across the northern regions of North America, Europe, and Asia. The long winters mean that these forests are often covered in snow, and the growing season for the trees is very short. Almost all boreal trees are conifers, with tough, needle-like leaves, and bear their seeds in cones. Most are evergreen, which means they keep their leaves year-round.

WORLD'S BIGGEST FOREST

The taiga, which is another word for boreal forest, stretches over 6,200 miles (10 000 kilometers) across the whole of northern Russia, from the Baltic Sea in the west to the Pacific Ocean in the east. Some of the world's longest rivers wind their way through the vast forest (below) to the Arctic Sea. North of the taiga is the frozen, treeless Arctic. South of the taiga are the warmer plains and grasslands of the Russian great steppes.

CANADA

CANADA'S forests stretch across the country, covering about half its land area. In many places, the forest (right) is broken up by lakes, as well as by the swampy ground called muskeg.

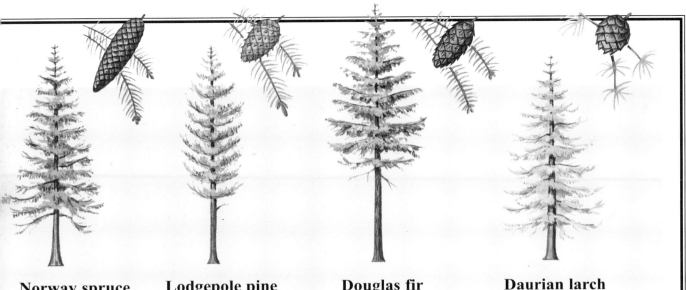

Norway spruce   **Lodgepole pine**   **Douglas fir**   **Daurian larch**

DIFFERENT CONIFERS
The conifers above belong to the pine family. They are evergreens except for larch, which drops its leaves in the fall.

GRIZZLY BEAR
Bears, beavers, moose, wolves, and foxes are among the larger animals of the boreal forest. North American grizzly bears seek out ice-cold rivers (right), where they can catch salmon swimming upstream to breed.

IN MILD ZONES

TEMPERATE FORESTS grow where the climate is mild, such as in parts of North America, Europe, and China. These places have warm summers, cool winters, and plenty of rain year-round.

Many temperate forests are full of deciduous broad-leaf trees, which shed their leaves each fall. The trees do this to save energy and moisture, and spend the winter as if they were asleep. They grow new leaves each spring. Temperate forests on steep slopes are usually made up of evergreen conifers.

REDWOODS

REDWOODS (left) are huge conifers that grow in temperate evergreen forests near the west coast of the USA. Redwoods are the world's tallest trees, and can grow to 328 feet (100 meters) high. These huge trees stop most of the sunlight from reaching the forest floor.

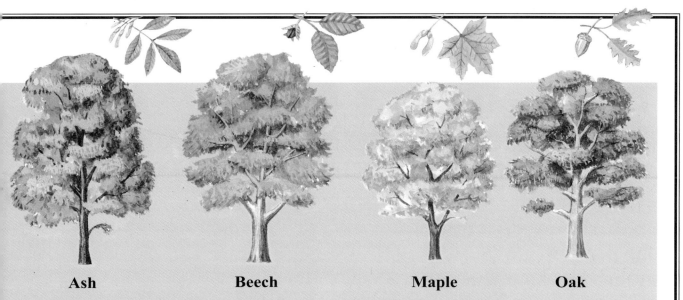

Ash **Beech** **Maple** **Oak**

FALL COLORS

As deciduous trees prepare for the winter, the green chlorophyll in their leaves fades. The chemical processes involved cause the trees, such as these in Maine, USA (left), to show the typical fall colors of red, yellow and brown.

BROAD-LEAF TREES

Most broad-leaf trees in temperate forests, such as ash, beech, maple, and oak, are deciduous (above). The leaves of many of them turn brilliant colors in the fall. In warm climates, some oak trees are evergreen.

EVERGREEN FOREST

The evergreen forests of New Zealand are home to rare flightless birds, such as kiwis (right). During the day, kiwis hide in burrows or among tree roots. They come out at night to find food – worms, insects, fruit, and leaves. The kiwi has no tail, and its stumpy wings are hidden in its hairy-looking feathers.

TROPICAL FORESTS

TROPICAL RAINFORESTS grow near the equator on warm, wet lowlands. Of all the world's forests, these have the greatest variety of trees. Most are broad-leaf evergreen trees, and many are up to 130 feet (40 meters) high. The forest's ground is covered by a thick undergrowth that we call jungle.

Other kinds of tropical forests, including some in Africa, India, and China, have both rainy and dry seasons each year.

RARE RHINOCEROS

Southeast Asian rainforests are home to the Sumatran rhino (below), sometimes called the hairy rhinoceros. These animals have been hunted for their horns and are now in danger of becoming extinct.

AMAZON RAINFOREST

THE thick forest around the Amazon River (left), in South America, forms the biggest rainforest in the world. Every day, however, parts of the forest are cut down to make way for farmland and roads (right).

BUTTRESS ROOTS

MANY of giant rainforest trees have huge buttress roots (above). These jut out from the lower part of the trunk to give the tree a wide base and so help support it.

PLANTS GROWING ON TREES

Epiphytes, or air plants, grow on tree branches without harming them. They are common in tropical forests. Epiphytes, such as these bromeliads (below) growing on a eucalyptus tree, have clusters of leaves that hold a lot of water. They sometimes grow in tiny pockets of soil that form in the bark of trees.

MOUNTAINS AND COASTS

IN THE mountains, it gets colder as you go higher. The changing temperatures affect mountain forests. Broad-leaf temperate forests grow on the foothills, but on higher, colder slopes, evergreen conifers grow instead. These conifer forests, such as those in the European Alps and southern parts of the Rockies, are similar to boreal forests.

Along the warm, muddy coasts of many tropical regions, belts of swampy mangrove forest grow. Mangroves are the only trees in the world that can grow in salt water.

TREE LINES

On tall mountains, there is a limit above which trees will not grow because of the cold. This limit is called the tree line, and it can be seen in the Swiss Alps (above). There are conifers up to the line, and a few tough grasses and plants above it. The peak of the Matterhorn, in the background, reaches 14,692 feet (4 478 meters). There is also a tree line in freezing northern regions, such as Siberia (left). North of the line is a cold, treeless zone called the tundra.

MANGROVE ROOTS

Mangroves have prop roots that curve down from their trunk (above). These roots are above the water level, and take in the air the trees need. The trees' main roots grow down into the swampy mud.

SNOW LEOPARD

The snow leopard (below) lives in the high mountains of the Himalayas. When winter comes and the weather turns even colder than usual, the snow leopard moves down to the lower forests. It hunts deer, goats, marmots, and other small animals.

GOSHAWK

Goshawks (above) are large birds of prey that live in the forests of North America, Europe, and Asia. With a wingspan of 4 feet (1.2 meters), goshawks fly fast among the trees after their prey of hares, squirrels, and birds. In mountain forests where snow lies in winter, goshawks are paler than those living further south.

FOREST LAYERS

TREES ARE not the only plants that grow in forests. Forests are made up of layers of plants. If enough sunlight reaches the forest floor, ferns and flowers grow, forming the herb layer. Taller shrubs, or woody plants, form the next layer up. Above is the understory, a layer of short or young trees. At the very top is the canopy, made by the tops of the tallest trees. It gets the most sunlight, and forms a roof over the other layers.

ON THE FOREST FLOOR

Many mushrooms and other fungi grow on the forest floor. Some, like the glistening ink-caps above, grow on the trunks and stumps of dead or dying trees.

Canopy

Understory

Shrub layer

Herb layer

Forest floor

TOWERING UP

THE layers of a temperate deciduous forest are shown left. If the forest has an open canopy, the shrub layer is often thick with bushes. Many of the trees that form the understory will eventually grow to reach the canopy. Many types of birds and animals live in the different forest layers.

RAINFOREST CANOPY

The canopy of a rainforest (above) usually has three layers. The trees of the upper canopy grow to about 130 feet (40 meters). A few may be even taller. The middle canopy usually reaches about 65 feet (20 meters), and the lower canopy about 33 feet (10 meters) above ground. The shrub and herb layers are usually thin because very little sunlight gets through the canopies.

BABY RACCOONS

MOST raccoons live in wooded areas, often in small family groups. They have strong, sharp claws, and spend much of their life climbing in trees. They make dens in hollow logs, stumps, or trees, and come out at night to hunt for their food. They eat nuts, fruit, and small animals, such as frogs and fish.

ANIMALS ON THE GROUND

JUST LIKE trees and plants, the animals that live in a forest vary according to what sort it is. In temperate regions, worms, snails, mites, ants, and beetles all feed on the leaves that fall from the trees. In rainforests, the floor is damp, so animals such as leeches, flatworms, and land crabs are common, as are many different frogs. In all forests, large animals feed on smaller ones, while leaves, fruit, and nuts are food for plant eaters.

FOREST ELEPHANT

African elephants (right) live in the forests and bushland of central and western Africa. Living among trees, elephants eat mainly leaves and fruits, as well as grass and roots. Sometimes they strip bark from a tree with their strong tusks for a quick snack.

ARMY ANTS

IN most forests, ants live on the ground in large groups called colonies. Army ants, such as the one left, are always on the move. They travel in columns through the Amazon rainforest, eating other insects and larger animals.

ELK

ELKS, or wapiti, are big North American deer that eat grass, leaves, and small plants. Males (right) have antlers, but the females do not. In winter, herds of elk move south to find more sheltered forests.

BADGERS

The Old World badger (below), found all over Europe and northern Asia, is larger than its American cousin. Badgers use their strong claws to dig long underground burrows, called setts, which they fill with bracken and other vegetation for bedding. They come out at night to feed on small rodents, worms, insects, nuts, and berries.

BIGGEST CAT

The Siberian tiger (above) lives in the forests of northeastern Asia. The biggest of all the big cats, its body is up to 9 feet (2.8 meters) long, with a tail about 3 feet (90 centimeters) in length. Its thick coat keeps it warm in the bitterly cold winters. Unfortunately, there are few of these cats left.

IN THE TREES

THERE IS a wealth of animal life in a forest's trees. Different kinds of birds live and nest in them – from toucans and macaws in rainforests to woodpeckers and owls in cooler wooded regions.

Some animals live only in certain areas. For example, the orangutan lives only in the rainforest on two Asian islands. The koala lives only in the eucalyptus trees of Australia.

TOUCAN

Different kinds of toucans (above) live in the rainforests of Central and South America. They use their huge bills to pick fruit and berries from tropical trees.

KOALA

ALTHOUGH they are often called koala bears, Australian koalas (left) are not bears. Koalas are marsupials, which means the female carries her young in a pouch. Koalas eat the leaves and shoots of certain eucalyptus trees. They only come down to the ground to move to another eucalyptus tree.

RED SQUIRREL

An American red squirrel grasps a branch with its strong paws (above). Squirrels help the forest by burying nuts. Many of these nuts grow into new trees.

TREE SNAKE

SOME snakes live in trees, using their tails to hang from branches. The eyelash viper (above) of Central America is about 20 inches (50 centimeters) long. It gets its name from the raised scales over its eyes.

ORANGUTAN

Orangutans (above) are the largest tree-dwelling mammals. They eat and sleep in the trees, swinging between branches to move through the rainforest. The orangutan's name means "man of the forest" in the Malay language.

CHIMPANZEE

Chimps live in the rainforests of Africa (right). Like orangutans, they are at home in the trees and sleep in nests made of branches. Chimps, however, spend more time on the ground, searching for food.

PEOPLE OF THE FOREST

THROUGHOUT THE centuries, people have lived in forests without destroying them. The Pygmies of central Africa, for example, have lived by hunting animals and gathering plants. Living in small groups, they move from camp to camp in search of food, building huts as they go.

Pygmies see the forest as the giver of life. It gives them food, clothing, and shelter, so they try not to harm it. Now, however, outsiders are cutting down the forests, destroying the Pygmies' home.

THE KAYAPO

This young Kayapo boy (below, center) holds a ceremonial headdress. The Kayapo live in the Amazon rainforest of Brazil. They grow maize and sweet potatoes in their forest villages. Like many other forest peoples, the Kayapo are losing their traditional land.

PYGMIES

Central African pygmies (below, left) build their huts of saplings and leaves. The Mbuti Pygmies of the Ituri forest are thought to be the shortest people in the world. Some adult women are just 4 feet (1.24 meters) tall.

IN THE WOODLANDS

THIS photograph, taken in the early 1900s, shows a Cree settlement in North America. Cree people once lived in the forests and woodlands of eastern Canada. Their tent homes, called tepees, were made of skin or bark stretched over wooden poles. Men hunted and fished, while women and children gathered roots, berries, fruits, and nuts in the forest.

FRUIT OF THE FOREST

The Dayak woman below is choosing jackfruit in the market. Many different Dayak groups live on the island of Borneo, in southeast Asia, which is part of Malaysia and part of Indonesia. Some Dayaks still live in their traditional longhouses, with up to 50 families per house.

USING WOOD

WE USE wood every day. In many parts of the world, wood is the main fuel for cooking and heating. It is used everywhere to make furniture and build homes. In factories, paper and plastics are just two of the things made from wood. Humans use up a huge number of trees! In managed forests, new trees are planted to replace those cut down. Replacement is only possible, however, when fast-growing conifers are planted.

WOOD MOUNTAIN
At the plant in Australia shown above, pine logs are cut up into tiny wood chips to be used for making paper or chipboard. The wood chips are piled high next to the plant.

LOGGING
When trees have been felled (right), the logs are taken to a sawmill. Today, this is usually done with cranes, tractors, and forklift trucks. If a river is nearby, the logs are floated to the sawmill.

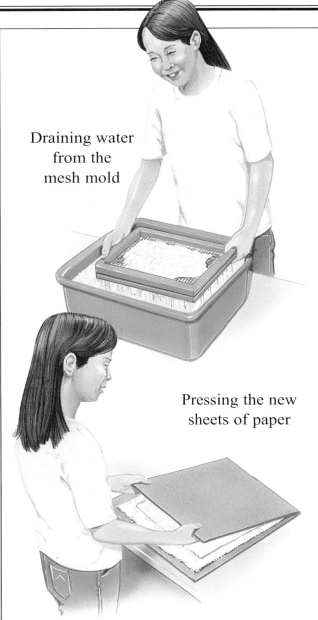

Draining water from the mesh mold

Pressing the new sheets of paper

RECYCLING PAPER

Recycling plants, such as the one in Indonesia shown below, turn paper back into pulp and make it into new paper. The plants serve two purposes — they reduce the number of trees we must cut down to produce the pulp from which paper is made. They also solve the problem of what to do with waste paper.

MAKING PAPER

THE Chinese invented paper over 2,000 years ago. They made pulp by mixing the bark of mulberry trees with water. Then they put it on a mesh mold and let it dry. We can still make paper in the same way today (above) as a craft or a hobby, but most paper is now made in large factories.

TODAY AND TOMORROW

MANY FORESTS are in danger. People cut down trees much faster than they plant them. Even when new trees are planted, it takes years for them to grow and replace those that were cut down in only a few minutes.

The clearing of forests is called deforestation. Fortunately, it is slowing down, but 115 square miles (300 square kilometers) of forest are still cut down every day. Rainforests are in the most danger, which means that everything that lives in them is also threatened.

FOREST ON FIRE

The great Amazon rainforest (above) has suffered more than most forests in recent years. Huge areas are burned to clear the land for cattle farming and to make roads to reach the interior of the forest.

SLASH AND BURN

PEOPLE in many countries burn patches of forest to grow their food. In Indonesia (left), big companies have done this, leaving dead forests and a smoky smog.

PLANNING FOR THE FUTURE

THOUGHT and planning are needed to preserve our forests. The scientist above is checking seedlings of different kinds of trees before they are planted in Mount Rainier National Park, USA. In protected areas such as this, visitors can enjoy the forest's natural beauty.

PROTECTING FOREST LIFE

PROTECTED areas can help stop the problems of deforestation. In Poland and Belarus, a national park of ancient spruce forest has been created to save the European bison (below), which was in danger of dying out.

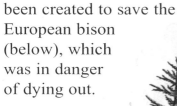

GLOSSARY

Amphibian	An animal that lives on land and breeds in water
Bird of prey	A bird that hunts animals and other birds for food
Boreal forest	A forest of the earth's northern regions, mainly made up of conifers
Broad-leaf tree	Any tree with wide, flat leaves instead of needles
Bushland	Land that is partly covered with shrubs and some small trees
Canopy	The top, leafy layer of trees in a forest
Chipboard	A building material made by pressing wood chips together
Chlorophyll	A green substance in plants that captures the energy in sunlight and helps to make the plants' food
Conifer	A tree with needle-like leaves that bears its seeds in cones. Most conifers are evergreen.
Deciduous	Describing trees that shed their leaves in the fall
Deforestation	The process of stripping the land of forests and trees
Epiphyte	A type of plant that grows on a tree without harming it
Equator	An imaginary circle that stretches around the middle of the earth
Evergreen	Describing trees that keep their leaves year-round
Extinct	Describing a type of animal that has died out
Glacier	A slowly moving mass of ice
Ice Age	A time when ice sheets covered large areas of the planet
Jungle	The thick, tangled undergrowth in a tropical forest

Jurassic   The period, over 140 million years ago, when dinosaurs lived on Earth

Marsupial   A type of mammal. Female marsupials carry their young in a pouch.

Mineral   A natural substance, such as salt, coal, or gold, found in the earth

Muskeg   A Canadian word for flat, swampy ground found in the North

Pulp   A soft, mushy substance made from wood, used in papermaking

Rainforest   A very wet, thick forest found in warm tropical areas

Recycle   To treat or break down waste material, such as glass, paper, or tin, so that it can be used again.

Scrubland   Dry land with tough bushes and short trees

Slash and burn   A method of clearing land for farming by cutting down trees and other plants and setting fire to them

Steppe   A Russian word for a flat grassy plain

Taiga   The huge boreal forest that stretches across northern Russia, between the tundra and the steppes.

Temperate forest   A forest, mainly made up of deciduous trees, found in the mild regions of the world

Tepee   A Native American tent home made of skin or bark

Tree line   The level on a mountain, or in far northern regions, beyond which no trees grow

Tropical   Describing something in the tropics, near the equator

Tundra   A cold, treeless part of the Arctic where the ground is always frozen beneath the surface

INDEX

A
Amazon rainforest 14, 20, 24, 28
army ants 20

B
badgers 21
bamboo 7
birds 13, 17, 22
bison 29
boreal forest 6, 10-11
broad-leaf trees 8, 12, 13, 14 16
bromeliads 15
buttress roots 15

C
canopy 18, 19
carbon dioxide 4, 5
chimpanzees 23
chipboard 26
chlorophyll 5, 13
coal 9
coastal forests 16, 17
conifers 4, 10-11, 12, 16, 26
Cree people 25

D
Dayak people 25
deforestation 28
dinosaurs 8

E
elephants 20
elk 21
epiphytes 15
eucalyptus 6, 15, 22

F
ferns 5, 8, 18
fruit 19, 20, 22

G
giant panda 7
grizzly bear 11

H
herb layer 18, 19

I
Ituri forest 24

J
jungle 14

K
Kayapo people 24
koala 22

L
logging 26

M
mangroves 16, 17
minerals 4, 5
moose 11
moss 5
mountain forests 16, 17
muskeg 10

N
nuts 19, 20, 22

O
orangutan 22, 23
oxygen 5

P
paper 26, 27
peat 9
Petrified Forest National Park 9
pine 11, 26
Pygmies 24

R
raccoons 19
rainforests 4, 14. 15, 19, 20, 22, 23, 28
recycling 27
red squirrel 22
redwoods 12
rhinoceros 14

S
shrub layer 18, 19
Siberian tiger 21
snow leopard 17
spruce 11, 29
swamp forests 8, 9

T
taiga 10
temperate forest 6, 12-13, 18, 20
tree line 16
tree snakes 23
tropical forests 14-15
tundra 16

U
understory 18

W
wapiti 21

1 2 3 4 5 6 7 8 9 0 Printed in the U.S.A. 7 6 5 4 3 2 1 0 9 8